To..

from..

'TO A VERY SPECIAL'® AND 'TO-GIVE-AND-TO-KEEP'® ARE
REGISTERED TRADE MARKS OF EXLEY PUBLICATIONS LTD AND
EXLEY PUBLICATIONS LLC.

OTHER BOOKS IN THE TO-GIVE-AND-TO-KEEP® SERIES:

Welcome to the New Baby	To a very special Dad
To a very special Daughter	To a very special Friend
To a very special Grandma	To a very special Granddaughter
To a very special Grandpa	To my very special Husband
Happy Anniversary	To someone very special
To my very special Love	Merry Christmas!
To a very special Mother	To a very special Sister
To a very special Son	To my very special Wife

Published simultaneously in 1997 by Exley Publications LLC in the
USA and Exley Publications Ltd in Great Britain.

12 11 10 9 8 7 6 5 4 3 2 1

Copyright © Helen Exley 1997, 2006
The moral right of the author has been asserted.
ISBN 1-86187-361-1

A copy of the CIP data is available from the British Library on request.
All rights reserved. No part of this publication may be reproduced or
transmitted in any form or by any means, electronic or mechanical,
including photocopy, recording or any information storage and retrieval
system without permission in writing from the Publisher.

Written by Pam Brown
Pam Brown published with permission © Helen Exley 1997
Edited by Helen Exley
Illustrated by Juliette Clarke
Printed in China

Exley Publications Ltd, 16 Chalk Hill, Watford, Herts WD19 4BG, UK.
Exley Publications LLC, 185 Main Street, Spencer, MA 01562, USA.
www.helenexleygiftbooks.com

To *a very special*®
MOTHER-IN-LAW

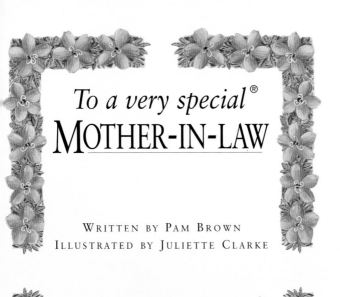

WRITTEN BY PAM BROWN
ILLUSTRATED BY JULIETTE CLARKE

A mother-in-law like you is one of
those glorious extras in life, that one
never dared hope for.

A HELEN EXLEY GIFTBOOK

▣ EXLEY

How good to have someone new to love
– and to love me in return.

…

I'll never forget the great surge of happy relief that
swept over me when first we met. They'd
said I'd love you. And I did.

…

Mothers and their children are bound by memories.
Their lives are so intertwined, their love
and their values are confused by the years they've
shared. But for a mother-in-law no past
recollections blur her feelings.
You see and love me as I am – *now*.

…

How often a mother-in-law has stepped into the
place of a mother lost or separated by great
distances.
Never becoming her
– but constant in love and understanding, patience
and enduring kindness.
A most dear friend.

…

A marriage can always do with some extra love
– and that is what you've given us.

…

One doesn't get to choose one's in-laws.
But if I had had the chance
I would have chosen you.

…

AT FIRST SIGHT

How warily we approached each other – neither
knowing quite what to expect. Eager to like.
To be liked. But half afraid.
How long ago that seems.
How glad I am you came from nowhere and linked
your life with mine.

…

One finds someone to share one's life
– but takes with them an obligatory gift
– a mother-in-law.
And some have wished they could refuse her!
But mine has proved a golden bonus to my joy –
a dear and wise companion.

…

"And this is my mother."

How did I know, then, that I was being
introduced to someone who was
to be one of my dearest friends: a sharer of
anxieties, a comforter in sorrow, a fellow hatcher
of most splendid plots – a galavanting
good companion?

...

The first meeting with one's prospective
mother-in-law is a terrifying experience.
For both of you.
And, oh, the blessed relief when you discover that
you *like* each other!

...

Happiness
is discovering
your in-laws are
wonderful.

...

MEETING 'THE FAMILY'

Exam results? First day in the new job?

Scary – but not so scary as Meeting The Family.

Mother looks brave and prepared for the worst.

Dad looks resigned.

Your eyes flicker about the room,

searching desperately

for clues. You discover your smile has stiffened

to a mask.

You make encouraging cat noises to a

fur hat. You drop your fork. And yes –

it's the washing-up that saves you.

"... And have you known him *long?*"

"... Don't bother with the saucepans, dear...

I'll do them later."

"... Come and see the garden."

"Do you garden at all?" "You *do*...."

You go home blurred, with your

arms full of cuttings.

And spinach.

The pattern has been set for a lifetime.

…

We find our friends in a thousand ways

– I found you when I married.

…

My best wedding present was my mother-in-law.

…

WISE AND UNDERSTANDING

Everyone needs someone kind and close and wise
to turn to when they are bewildered.
Thank heavens for mothers, but thank heavens too
for mothers-in-law who add another
dimension to our understanding.

...

You came into my life – and brought with you
the experience of your lifetime, to
enrich my days.

...

You never dictate. You never criticize.
But you have given me, very quietly,
such *very* good advice.

...

You know when to take our troubles
very, very seriously
– and when to smile, and show us just how silly
we are being.

…

You are a wise woman – but not *too* wise,
thank heavens.
You can still turn to me for advice sometimes!
And that is just right.

…

Sometimes we squabble when you're around.
You say not a thing,
but the hurt and sorrow in your eyes brings
us to our senses.

…

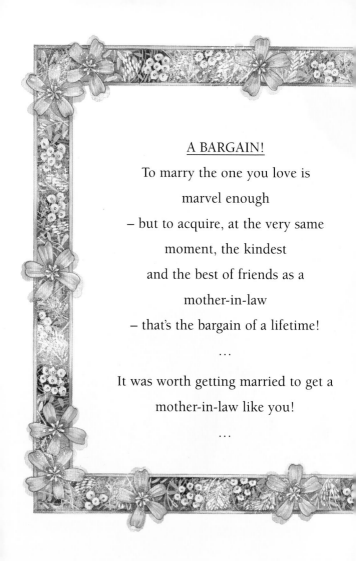

A BARGAIN!

To marry the one you love is
marvel enough
– but to acquire, at the very same
moment, the kindest
and the best of friends as a
mother-in-law
– that's the bargain of a lifetime!

...

It was worth getting married to get a
mother-in-law like you!

...

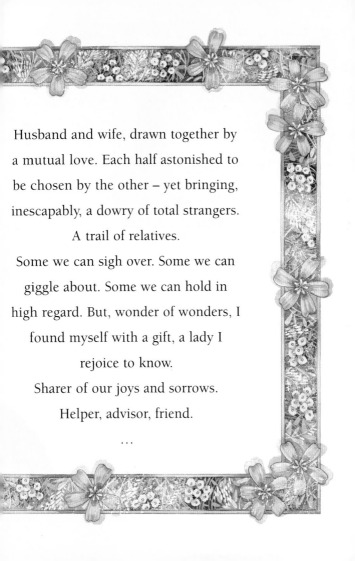

Husband and wife, drawn together by
a mutual love. Each half astonished to
be chosen by the other – yet bringing,
inescapably, a dowry of total strangers.

A trail of relatives.

Some we can sigh over. Some we can
giggle about. Some we can hold in
high regard. But, wonder of wonders, I
found myself with a gift, a lady I
rejoice to know.

Sharer of our joys and sorrows.

Helper, advisor, friend.

...

GOOD MOTHERS-IN-LAW...

... only give their recipes if they are asked,

know full well their child is by no means perfect,

never disrupt your plans,

never turn up without warning,

never expect to be told every move you

intend to make,

never run their dust-hunting fingers along surfaces

or inspect the oven,

quietly register the things you are desperately

in need of – and accidentally

"find" them in sales.

Who baby-sits at short notice, when it really is totally inconvenient? Who can diagnose rubella before the doctor? Who knows how to get Burgundy stains off the hand-sewn tablecloth? Who never takes sides – unless it's absolutely imperative. And does not necessarily side with their own child? Who doesn't give the children forbidden sweeties? Who leaves short sensible messages on the answer-phone?

Who always knows *exactly* the present everybody longs for?

Who is infinitely patient with the children – but knows when the time has come to Put Their Foot Down? Who keeps clear of family rows? Who looks after the cat when one's away?

You do!

...

THOSE NASTY JOKES

One would think the world is full of those mothers-
in-law so cherished by comedians – ugly,
lazy, greedy, selfish, domineering. How restricted
their patter would be if they acknowledged
the truth... the caring mothers-in-law all
over the world.

…

Whenever I hear yet another mother-in-law joke I
huff a little – remembering all the wonderful
mothers-in-law.
And, most particularly, you.

…

There are, of course, mothers-in-law from hell.

Those who disapprove of you on sight and never see any reason to revise their opinion.

Those who don't like the way you cook – anything.

Those who run their fingers along the top of shelves.

Those who say they'll give you a little present, as long as you buy A Three

Piece Suite.

Those who believe in senna pods.

I've <u>heard</u> about them.

How smug I feel!

...

TWO FAMILIES BECOME ONE

There we were – two totally different families, each
with their own eccentricities,
ambitions, fears, excitements and contentments.
But now, because two people love each other, we are
one – new friendships made, new
alliances created. The world has expanded for us all.
And we two, who brought you all together,
congratulate ourselves, we have
transformed an excellent short story into a saga!!!

…

You took me by the hand to an open door, into a
place of warmth and light and smiling faces.
This is your new family, you said.
And so it was.

…

You two sit by my bed, enraptured by the
baby... the generations linked by love.

…

Dear Mother-in-law, you are the thread
that links the fabric of my family to
your own.
We stitch the world,
the generations, the lives of individuals,
together – so that every person in both of our
families is part of one rich fabric.
Beige and scarlet, turquoise, indigo, silk and
cotton – a million, million lives – and a few,
like you, of purest gold.

...

LINKED BY LOVE

We love your child – but that does not
stop us from sometimes catching each other's
eye and giving an amused and
sympathetic wink!

…

We met a little warily –
you wondering if I was good enough for your child,
myself recalling all the tales of dreadful
mothers-in-law.
But we talked and smiled
– and shared a fund of mischievous tales
about your child, our common love.
And became friends,
our lives interlinked
and richer for the friendship.

…

A good mother-in-law loves her child – but knows
all the foibles and the weaknesses.
And so holds neutral ground.

…

We know your child so well, you and I.
We share the exasperation and the smiles.
Companions in affection. Partners in aggravation.
Linked by love.

…

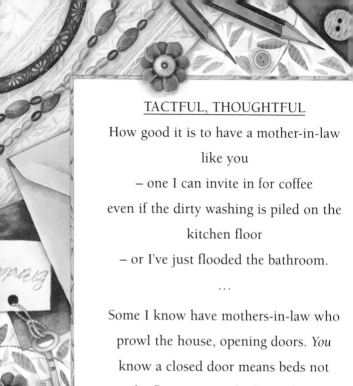

TACTFUL, THOUGHTFUL

How good it is to have a mother-in-law
like you
– one I can invite in for coffee
even if the dirty washing is piled on the
kitchen floor
– or I've just flooded the bathroom.

...

Some I know have mothers-in-law who
prowl the house, opening doors. *You*
know a closed door means beds not
made, floors not washed – or drawers
being sorted through all over
the carpet.

...

You are that gem among mothers-in-law
– you never look for dust.

...

There is nothing so discreet as a wise
mother-in-law.

...

You have a genius for not phoning in
the middle of a TV serial.

...

Mothers and mothers-in-law know
more than you suspect.
It is very difficult to astonish them.

...

If you ever need
an extra pair of hands –
just whistle and I'll come.
It's only fair.
You've done so much for me.

…

THANK YOU!

For hot buttered scones and cups of tea, for loans
of bus fares, sugar, bird seed, for hugs and
scoldings, for a shoulder to cry on,
for great things and little things
– for making this world a happier place
– our thanks!

…

You don't blanch when you walk into a domestic
emergency.
You grab a mop – or a towel – or a spanner.
And tell me about the disasters you have dealt with:
flaming toast, drunken spin-driers....

…

You are the perfect mother-in-law. You help wrestle
the cat into the cat box for a trip to the vet. You get
in the washing when it starts to pour with rain.
You dry as I wash up.
You make your visits times to relish.

…

All wives, and husbands, are not wonderful at
everything. But, bound by love, their mothers
and their spouses applaud the effort that went into
the rock-hard scones, the drunken shelving.
They see the goodwill behind the
slightly defective effort.

…

LOVE

We talked of you, long before you and I met, with
such pleasure, such affection.
And now I know why.

...

I love you because you are you.
Because you never interfere – but are there
when I most need you.
Because you share the love I have for your dear
child – and the exasperation.
Because something of you is in them.
and something of them is in you.
Because you are my friend.

...

Marriage gave me,
against all my expectations,
someone extra to love.

...